3

american popular piano

REPERTOIRE

Compositions by
Christopher Norton

Additional Compositions
and Arrangements
Dr. Scott McBride Smith

Editor
Dr. Scott McBride Smith

Associate Editor
Clarke MacIntosh

NV Music

Book Design & Engraving
Andrew Jones

Cover Design
Wagner Design

A Note about this Book

Pop music styles can be grouped into three broad categories:

- **lyrical** — pieces with a beautiful singing quality and rich harmonies; usually played at a slow tempo;

- **rhythmic** — more up-tempo pieces, with energetic, catchy rhythms; these often have a driving left hand part;

- **ensemble** — works meant to be played with other musicians, or with backing tracks (or both!); this type of piece requires careful listening and shared energy.

American Popular Piano has been deliberately designed to develop skills in all three areas.

You can integrate the cool, motivating pieces in **American Popular Piano** into your piano studies in several ways.

- pick a piece you like and learn it; when you're done, pick another!

- choose a piece from each category to develop a complete range of skills in your playing;

- polish a particular favorite for your local festival or competition. Works from **American Popular Piano** are featured on the lists of required pieces for many festivals and competitions;

- use the pieces as optional contemporary selections in music examinations;

- Or...just have fun!

Going hand-in-hand with the repertoire in **American Popular Piano** are the innovative **Etudes Albums** and **Skills Books**, designed to enhance each student's musical experience by building technical and aural skills.

- **Technical Etudes** in both Classical and Pop Styles are based on musical ideas and technical challenges drawn from the repertoire. Practice these to improve your chops!

- **Improvisation Etudes** offer an exciting new approach to improvisation that guides students effortlessly into spontaneous creativity. Not only does the user-friendly module structure integrate smoothly into traditional lessons, it opens up a whole new understanding of the repertoire being studied.

- **Skills Books** help students develop key supporting skills in sight-reading, ear-training and technic; presented in complementary study modules that are both practical and effective.

Use all of the elements of **American Popular Piano** together to incorporate a comprehensive course of study into your everyday routine. The carefully thought-out pacing makes learning almost effortless. Making music and real progress has never been so much fun!

Library and Archives Canada Cataloguing in Publication

Norton, Christopher, 1953-

American popular piano [music] : repertoire / compositions by Christopher Norton ;
additional compositions and arrangements, Scott McBride Smith ;
editor, Scott McBride Smith ; associate editor, S. Clarke MacIntosh.

To be complete in 11 volumes.
The series is organized in 11 levels, from preparatory to level 10, each including a repertoire album,
an etudes album, a skills book, and an instrumental backings compact disc.

ISBN 1-897379-00-5 (preparatory level).--ISBN 1-897379-01-3 (level 1).--
ISBN 1-897379-02-1 (level 2).--ISBN 1-897379-03-X (level 3).--
ISBN 1-897379-04-8 (level 4).--ISBN 1-897379-05-6 (level 5)

1. Piano music--Teaching pieces. I. Smith, Scott McBride II. MacIntosh, S. Clarke, 1959- III. Title.

MT242.N883A52 2006   786.2   C2006-906213-7

LEVEL 3 REPERTOIRE

Table of Contents

POP BALLAD

Lonely Cottage

Christopher Norton

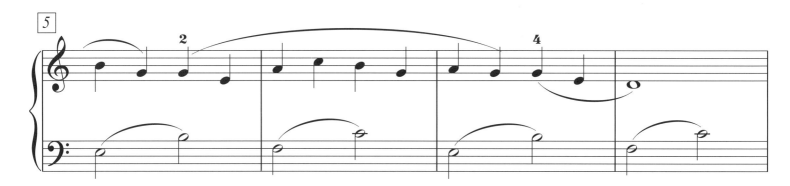

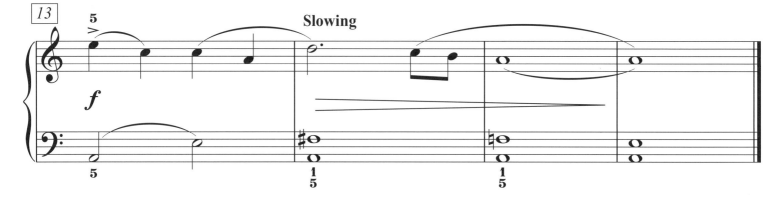

8-Beat Ballad

Drifting Away

Christopher Norton

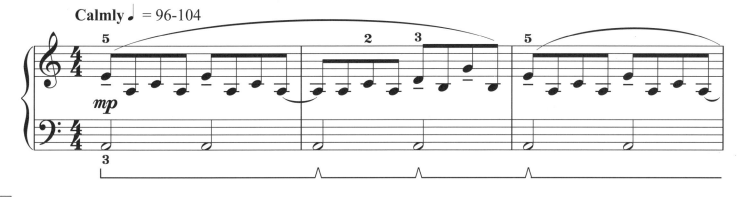

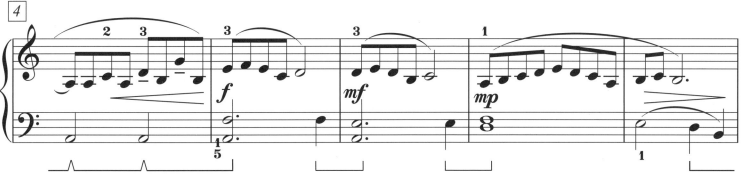

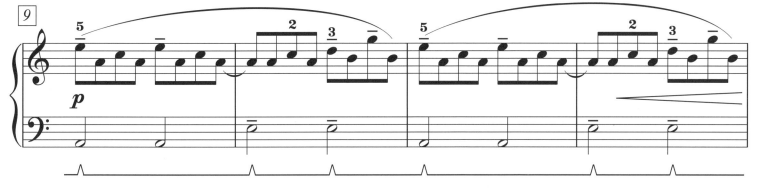

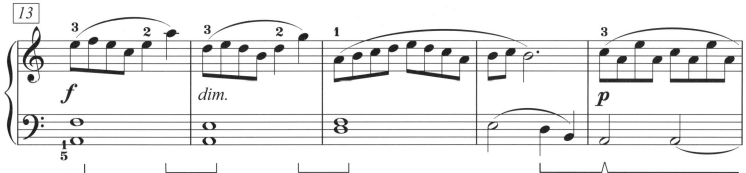

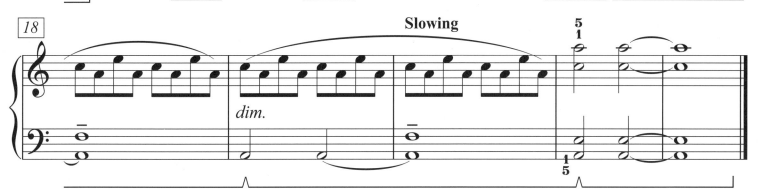

Family Holiday

Christopher Norton

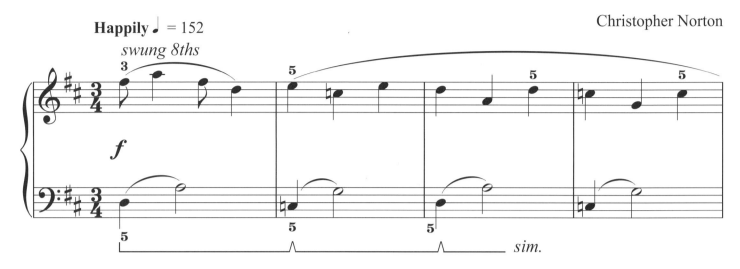

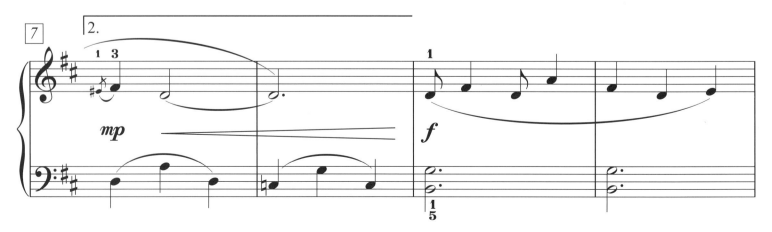

11
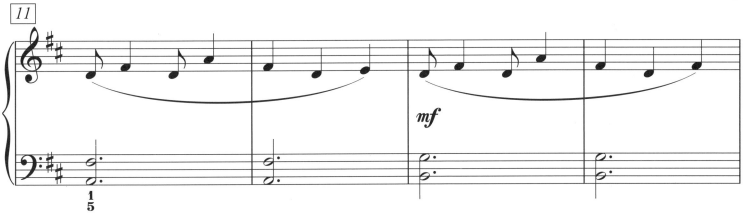

15
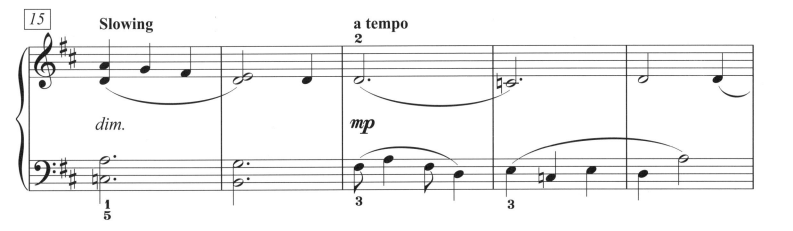

20
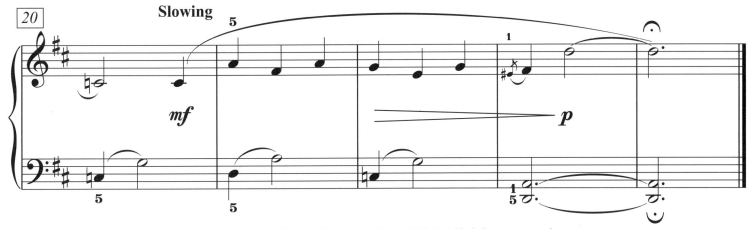

CHARACTER PIECE

Petals

Christopher Norton

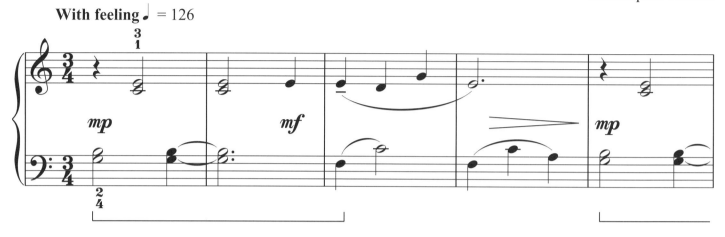

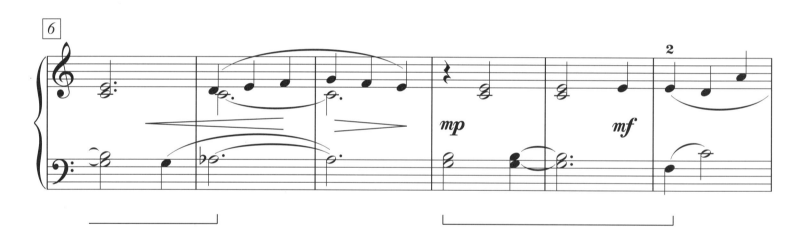

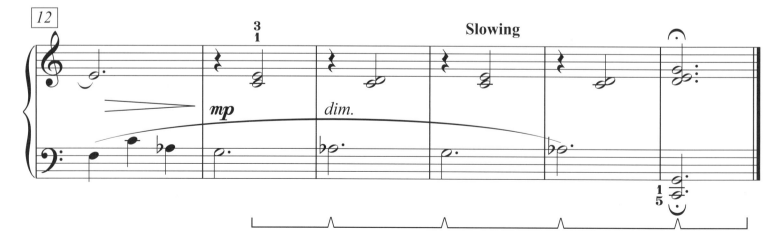

Doleful

WALTZ

Christopher Norton

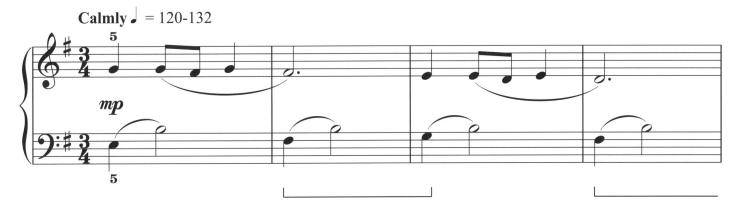

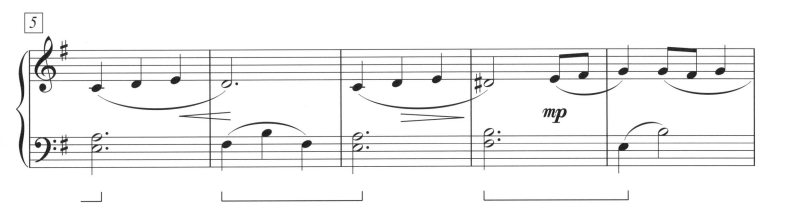

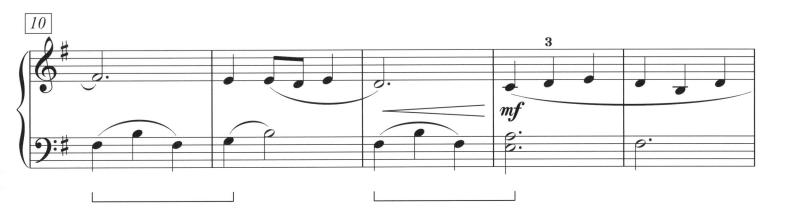

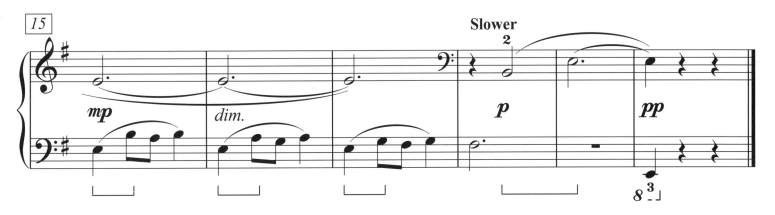

8

BOLERO

Snake Pit

Christopher Norton

Mysteriously ♩ = 132

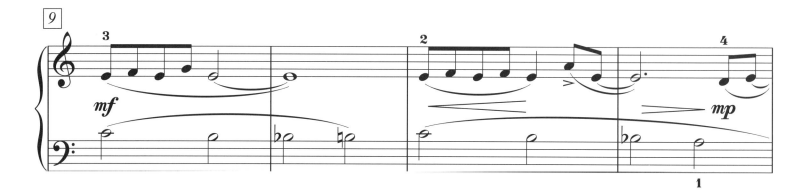

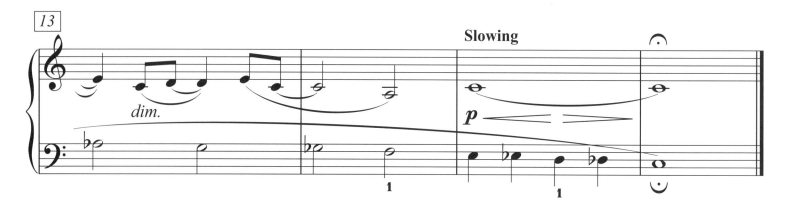

A Conversation

8-Beat Ballad

Christopher Norton

Expressively ♩ = 72-96

WALTZ

Sunny Disposition

Christopher Norton

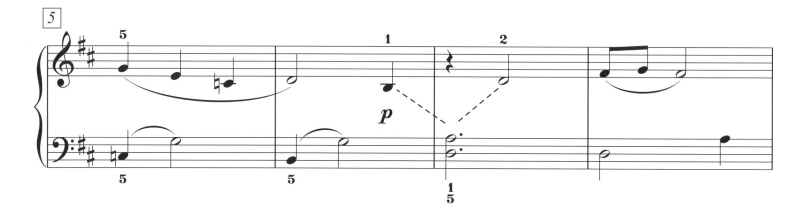

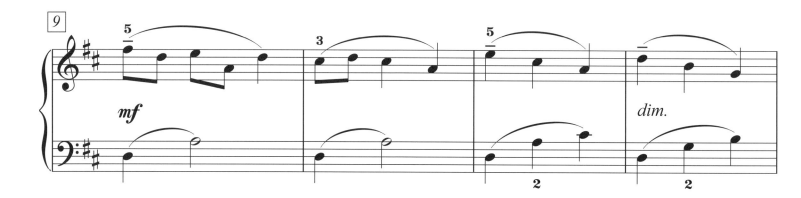

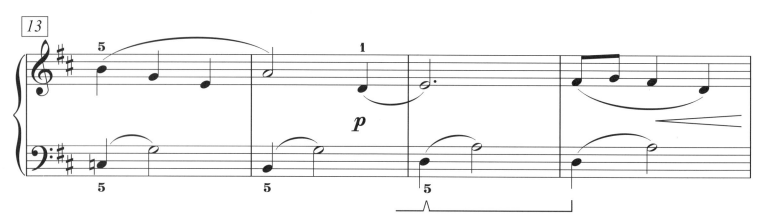

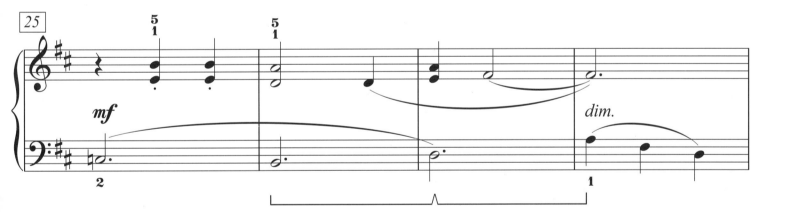

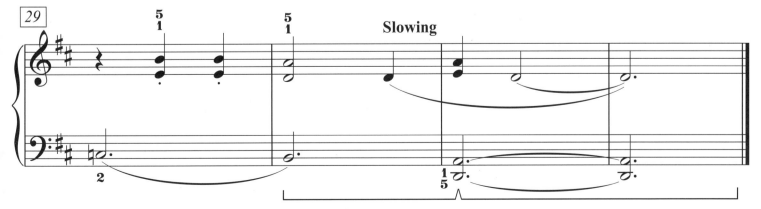

8-BEAT ROCK

War Dance

Christopher Norton

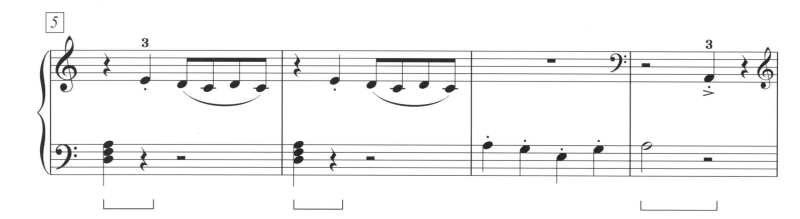

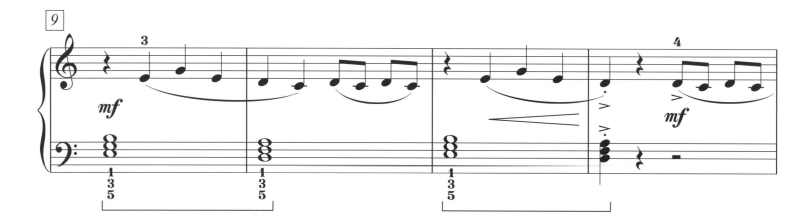

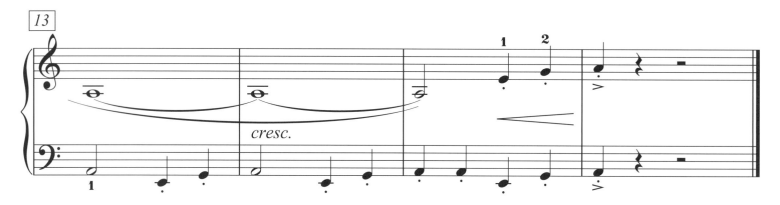

SWING

Puffed Up

Christopher Norton

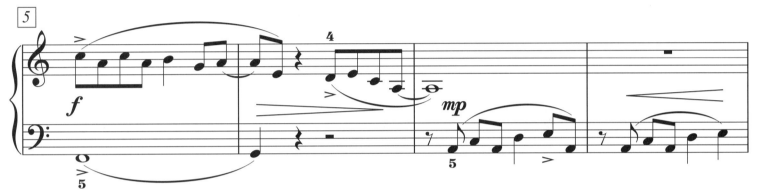

MARCH

Flag Waving

Christopher Norton

Cheerfully ♩ = 92

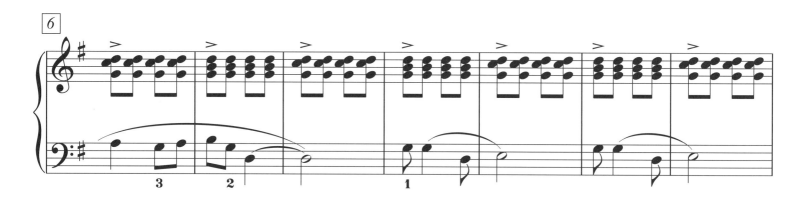

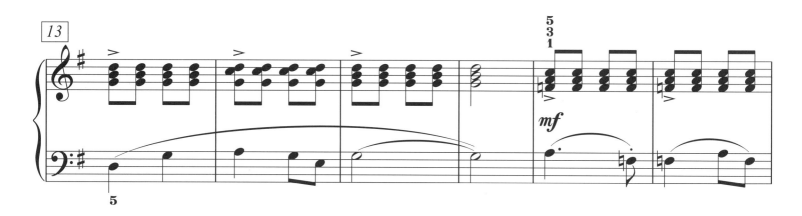

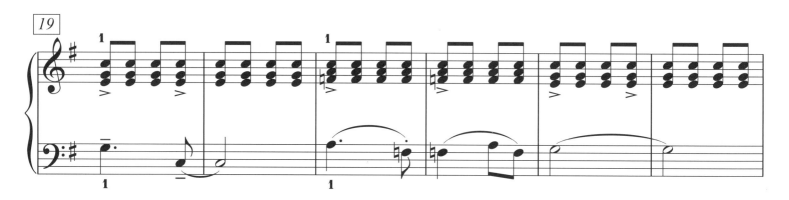

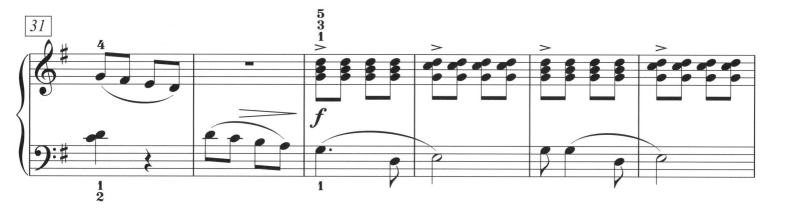

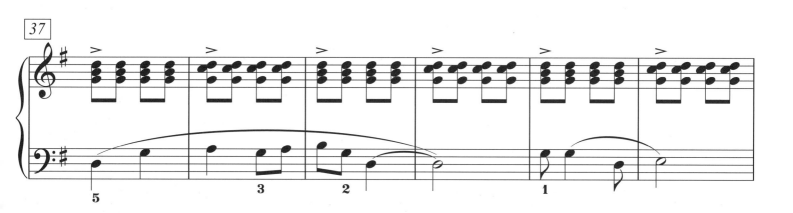

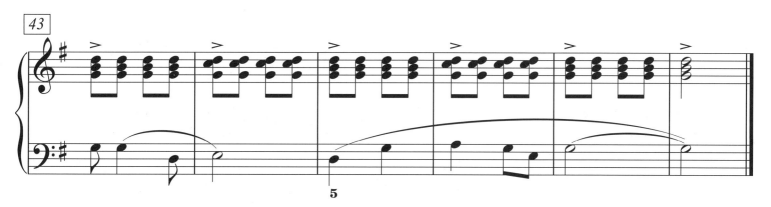

FANFARE

A Fanfare

Christopher Norton

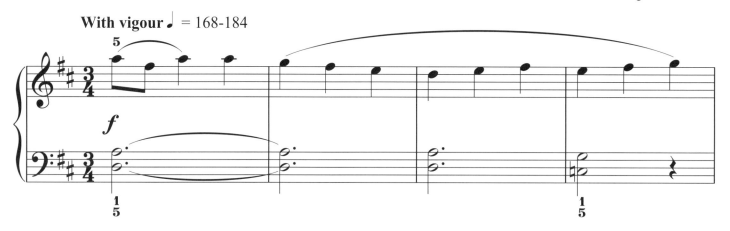

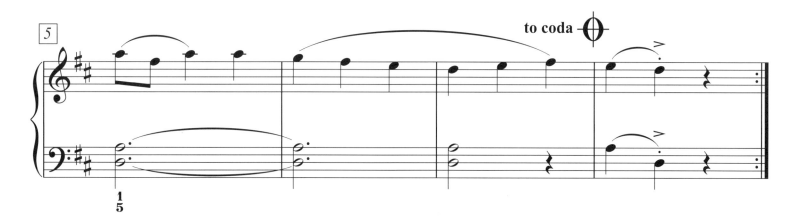

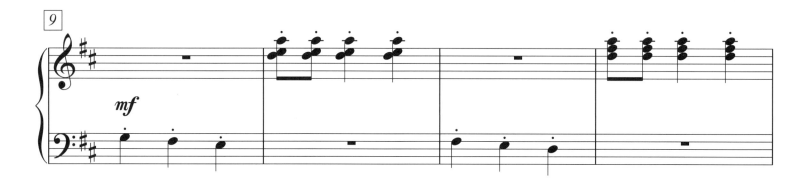

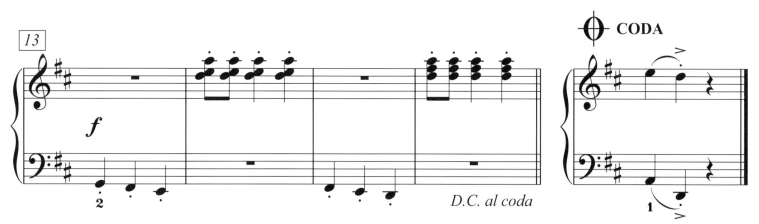

Motor City

Christopher Norton

MOTOWN

Firmly ♩ = 100

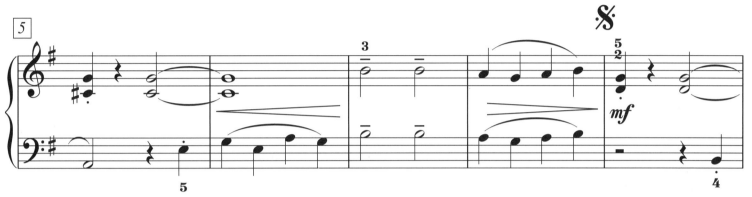

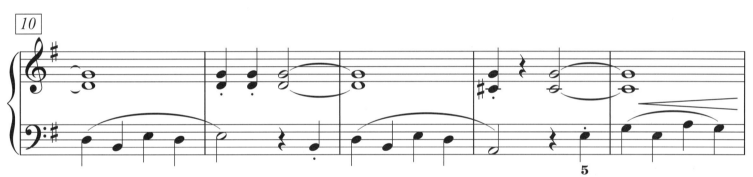

FINE

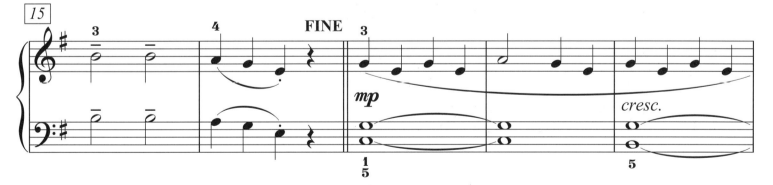

rh up *8ve* second time

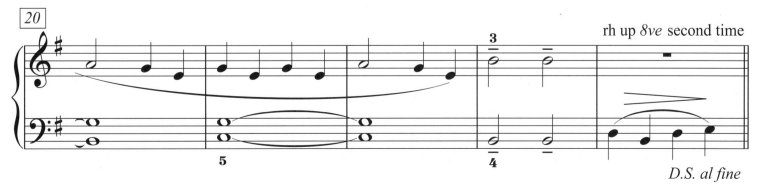

D.S. al fine

Getting To It

Christopher Norton

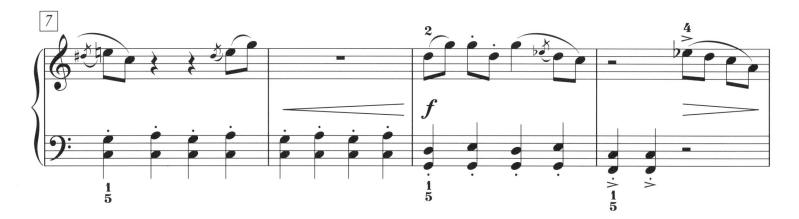

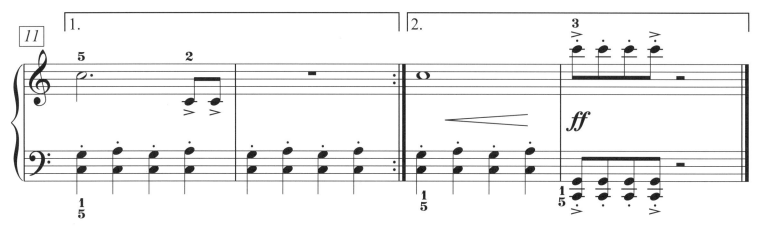

Spider Blues

Christopher Norton

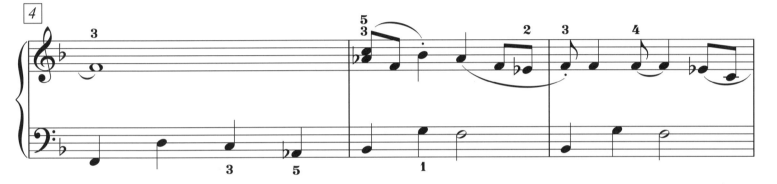

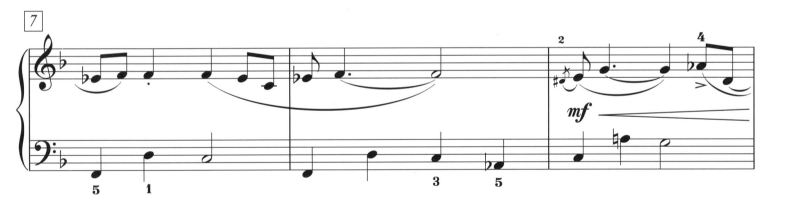

8-BEAT ROCK

All Over Town

Christopher Norton

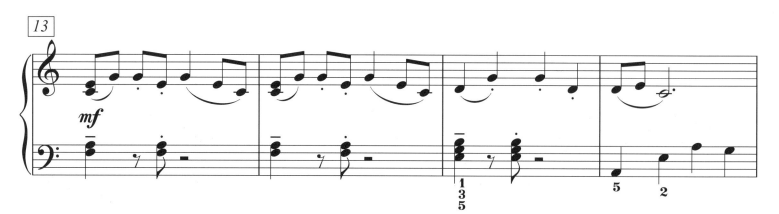

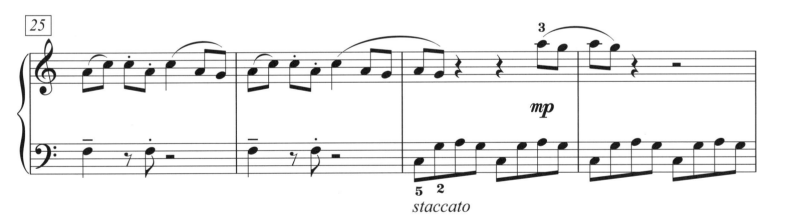

Celtic Caper

IRISH JIG

Christopher Norton

When played on one piano,
Piano Solo plays one octave higher.

Extrovertly ♩ = 132
swung 8ths

mf

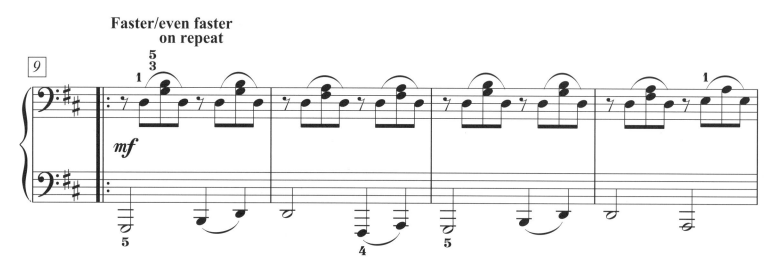

*Faster/even faster
on repeat*

mf

PIANO SOLO

Celtic Caper

Christopher Norton

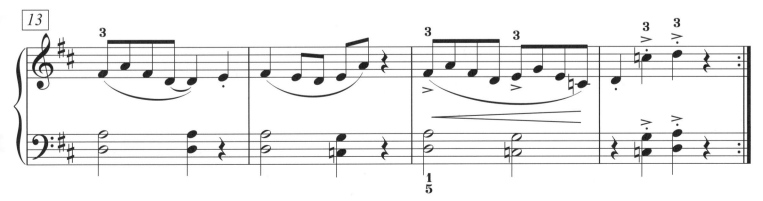

Jamaican Market

REGGAE

When played on one piano,
Piano Solo plays one octave higher.

Christopher Norton

Lightly, reggae style ♩ = 116

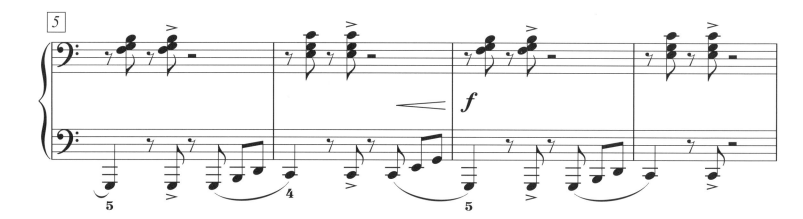

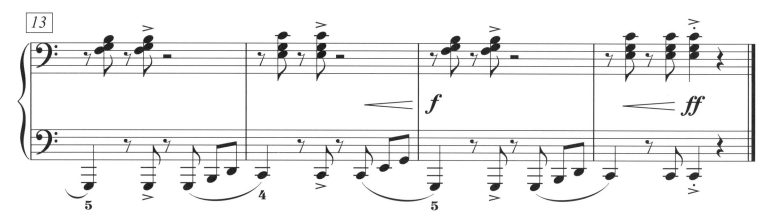

Jamaican Market

Christopher Norton

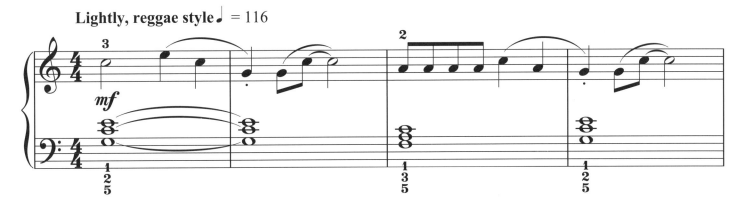

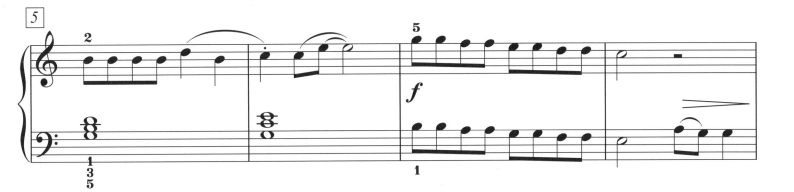

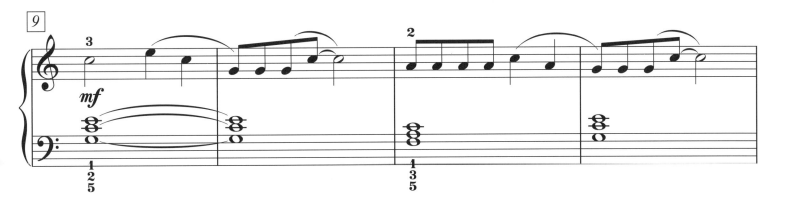

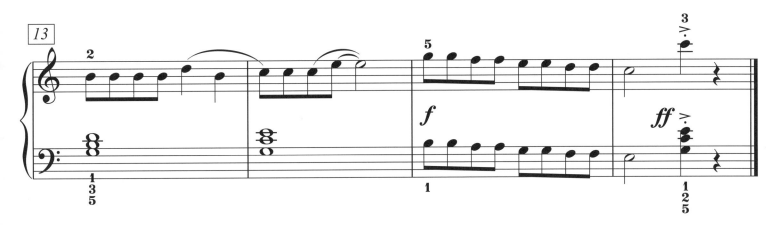

KC Shuffle

When played on one piano,
Piano Solo plays one octave higher.

Christopher Norton

Bouncy ♩ = 112

swung 8ths

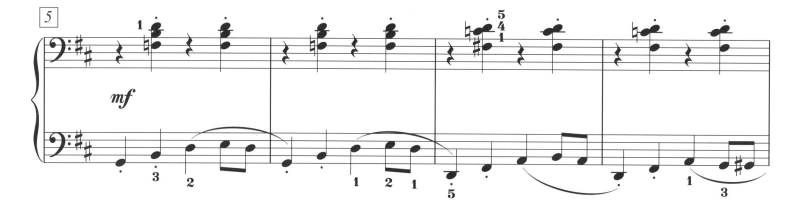

PIANO SOLO

KC Shuffle

Christopher Norton

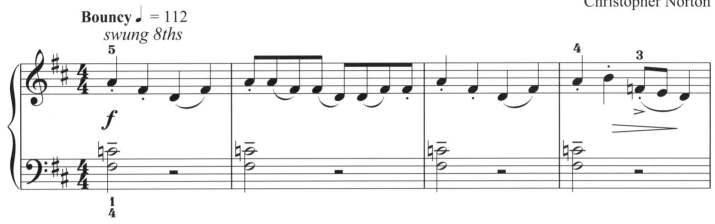

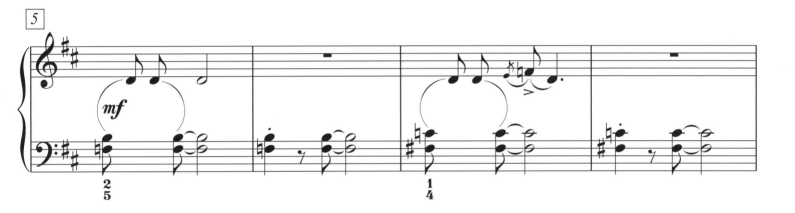

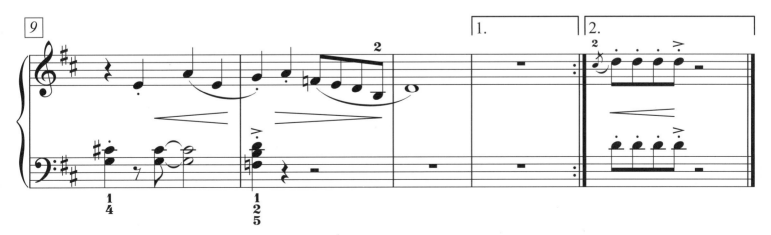

Corn Fed

When played on one piano,
Piano Solo plays one octave higher.

Christopher Norton

Easygoing ♩ = 126

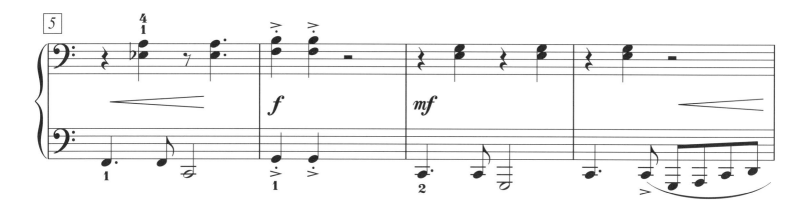

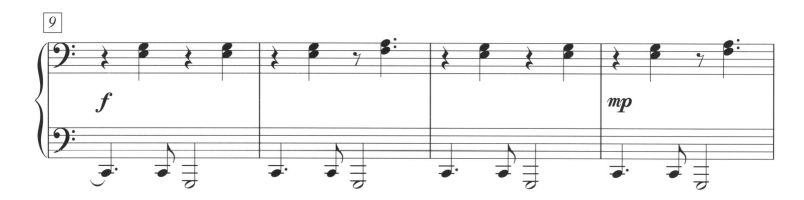

PIANO SOLO

Corn Fed

Christopher Norton

COUNTRY ROCK

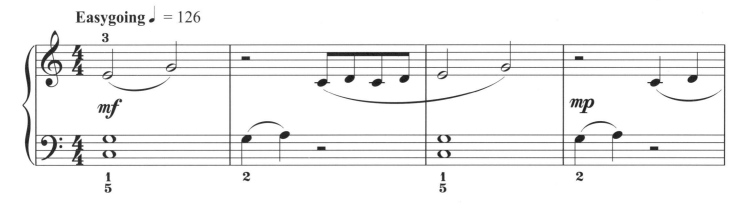

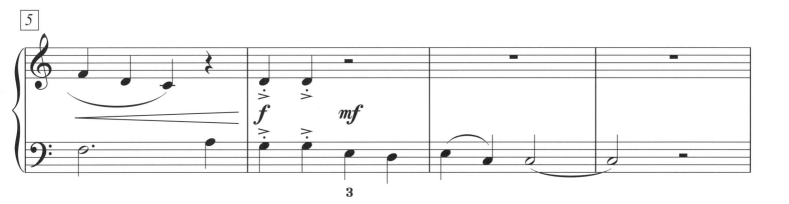

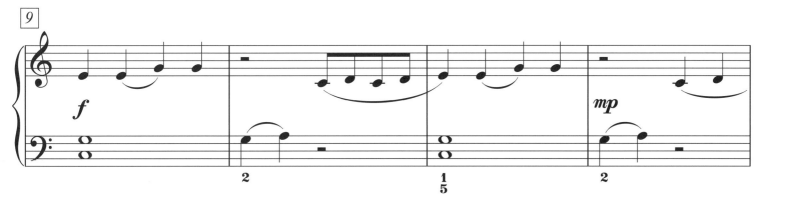

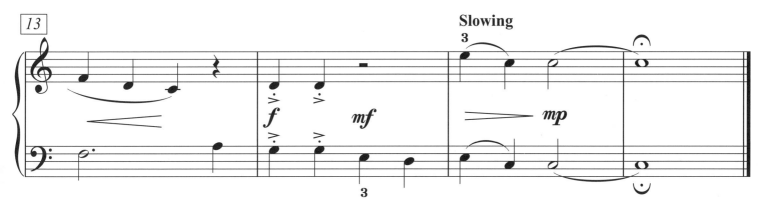

Boat Blues

When played on one piano,
Piano Solo plays one octave higher.

Christopher Norton

Toot that horn ♩ = 112

PIANO SOLO

Boat Blues

MANCINI BOOGIE

Christopher Norton

Toot that horn ♩ = 112

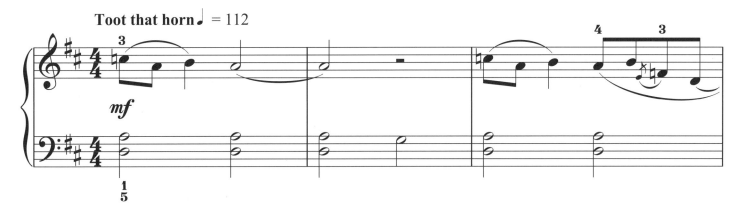

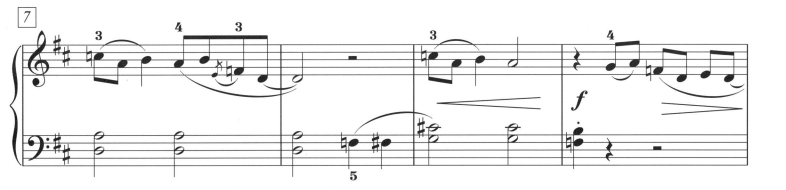

Lapping It Up

SOUL

When played on one piano,
Piano Solo plays one octave higher.

Christopher Norton

Rhythmically ♩ = 126

PIANO SOLO

Lapping It Up

SOUL

Christopher Norton

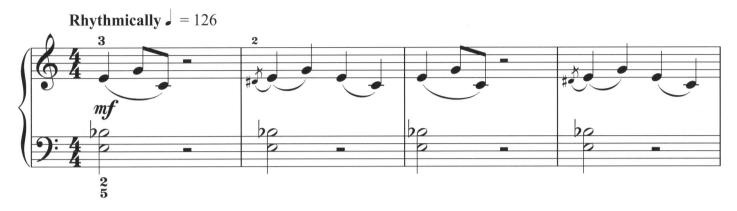

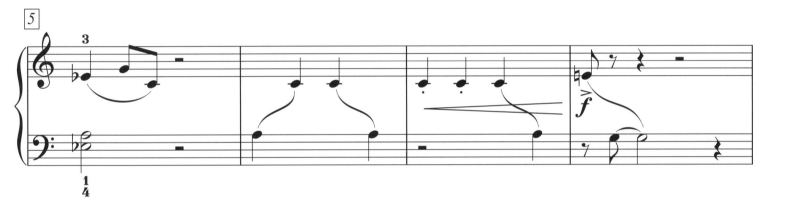

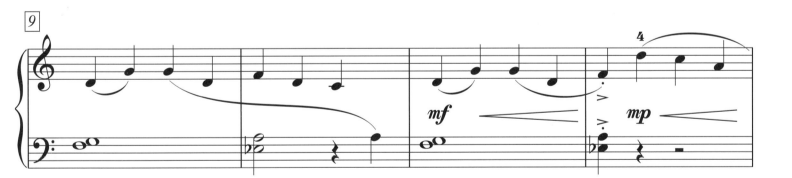

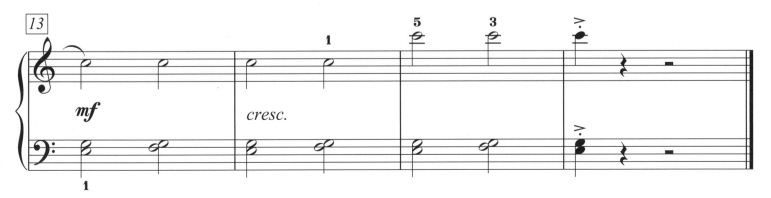

Country Boy

When played on one piano,
Piano Solo plays as written.

Christopher Norton

Relaxed ♩ = 132

swung 8ths

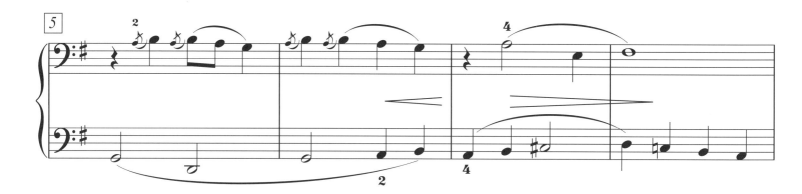

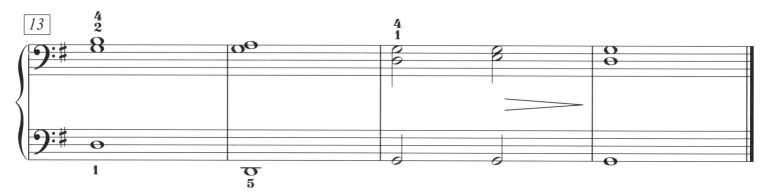

PIANO SOLO

Country Boy

COUNTRY SWING

Christopher Norton

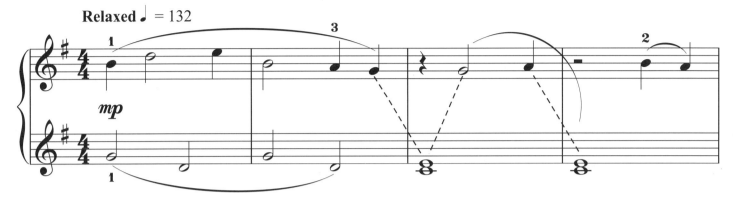

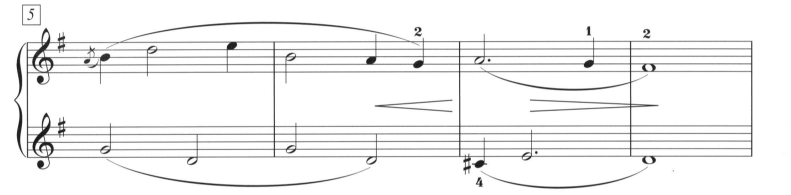

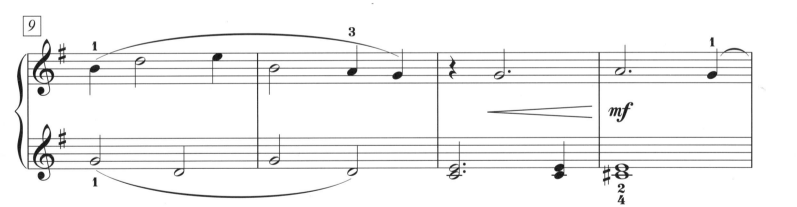

Tango Of The Desert

When played on one piano,
Piano Solo plays as written.

Christopher Norton

With spirit ♩ = 132

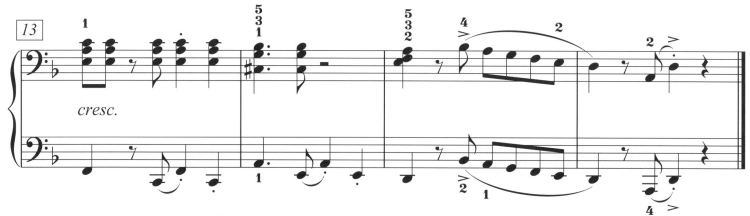

PIANO SOLO

Tango Of The Desert

Christopher Norton

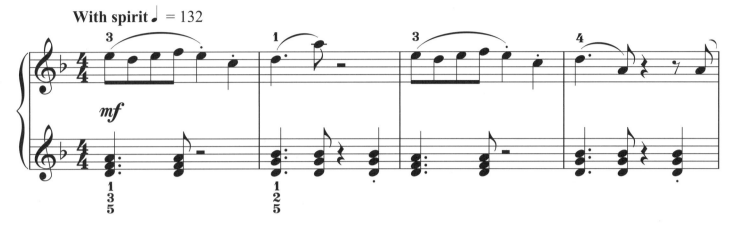

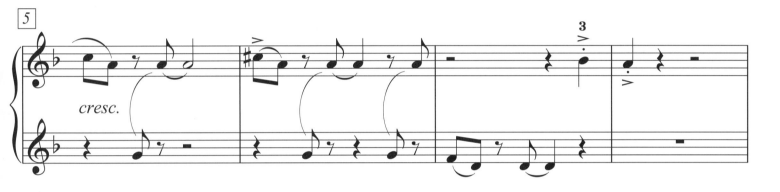

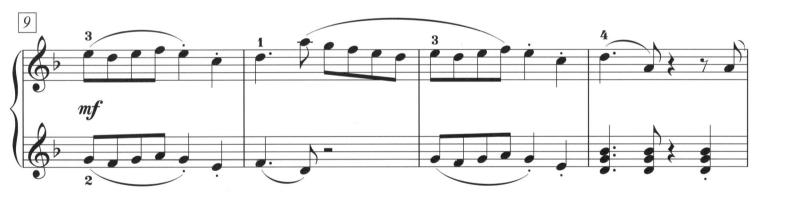

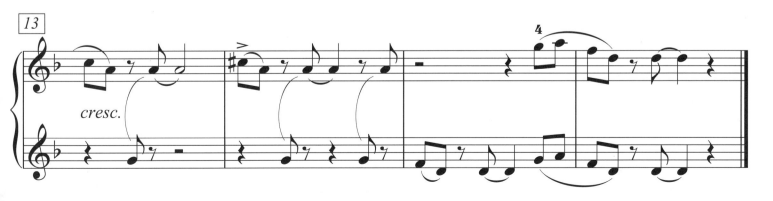

LEVEL 3 REPERTOIRE
Glossary

Symbols

♪ . . . . **Grace note** a note printed in small size, always played quickly in pop music.

⌒ . . . . **Slur** play the notes under or over the slur legato. Sometimes, the last note of a slur is shortened a bit.

Tenuto has two meanings:
1) emphasize the note a little bit;
2) hold the note for its full length, without connecting it to the following note. It could have either or both meanings—it is up to the performer to decide.

Terms and Forms

a tempo . . . . Return to the original tempo.

Backbeat . . . . Emphasis on beats 2 and 4, in a 4-beat bar. Usually accented by the drums, the backbeat is the most common rhythmic pattern in rock music.

Blues . . . . Musical genre created by African-American musicians, with "blues" notes played against a major-key chord progression. Examples include: *Spider Blues*

Blues notes . . . . A pattern based on a major scale with lowered 3rd, 5th, and 7th notes.

Bolero . . . . Refers to several types of Latin dance, usually slow and accompanied by castanets and acoustic guitar. Examples include: *Snake Pit*

Boogie . . . . Often found in rock and country music. The left hand plays a pattern of 5ths and 6ths while the right hand plays simple, bluesy licks. Examples include: *Getting To It*

Call and . . . . A style of singing in which
response the melody sung by one singer is echoed or "answered" by another. Examples include: *My Generation*

Calypso . . . . A popular song form from the Caribbean island of Trinidad, generally upbeat. Examples include: *Yellow Bird*

Character . . . . . . An evocative style based on a
piece single idea designed to create an atmosphere or picture in the listener's mind. Examples include: *Petals*

Coda . . . . "Tail". In music, it means an ending section.

Country rock . . . A combination of rock – with electric guitars, bass, drums, and a strong backbeat – and country stylings. Examples include: *Corn Fed*

Country . . . . A combination of country,
swing cowboy, polka, and folk music, blended with a jazzy "swing", featuring pedal steel guitar. Examples include: *Country Boy*

Da Capo . . . . "The head". It means go back to
(D.C.) the beginning and play again.

Dal Segno . . . . . . "From the sign". Look for the 𝄋
(D.S.) sign and repeat from that spot.

8-beat ballad . . . A slow to medium tempo sentimental popular song with 8 straight 8th notes per measure. Examples include: *A Conversation*

8-beat rock . . . . A staple rock 'n' roll rhythmic pattern with 8 eigth notes in every bar featuring a strong backbeat. Examples include: *All Over Town*

Fanfare . . . . A loud flourish of brass instruments, especially trumpets. Examples include: *Fanfare, Fanfare for the Common Man*

Fine . . . . End.

Form . . . . The arrangement of patterns in a piece, often based on repetition. **ABA** is a three-part form. The first section repeats at the end, with a contrasted section in the middle.

Gospel . . . . Religious music whose lyrics express spiritual belief. There are several types, often featuring a richly ornamented solo melody, accompanied by full harmonies. Examples include: *Nobody Knows The Trouble I've Seen*

Interval . . . . The distance from one note to another. **Harmonic intervals** two notes played at the same time. **Melodic intervals** two notes played one after the other.

Irish Jig . . . . A lively dance in triple feel, generally led by tin whistle and fiddle. Examples include: *Celtic Caper, The Rambler*

Jazz waltz . . . . . . A generally relaxed swing style in 3/4 time. Examples include: *Family Holiday*

Legato . . . . Smooth and connected.

loco . . . . Return to normal position.

Mancini . . . . A variation on the standard
boogie boogie left hand, made famous by Henry Mancini's *Baby Elephant Walk*. Examples include: *Boat Blues*

Motif . . . . A musical idea. It may consist of a short melody, a short rhythmic pattern, or both.

Motown . . . . A style of music which originated in Detroit, whose features include the use of tambourine along with drums and a "call and response" singing style derived from gospel music. Examples include: *Motor City, ABC*

Off-beat . . . . An accented note, motif, or phrase played on a normally unaccented beat.

Pop ballad . . . . . A form of slow love song prevalent in nearly all genres of popular music. There is generally an emphasis on romance in the lyrics. Examples include: *Lonely Cottage*

Reggae . . . . A music style from Jamaica, with elements of calypso, rhythm and blues, and characterized by a strong backbeat. Examples include: *Jamaican Market*

Rhythm . . . . A style of music that combines
and blues blues and jazz, characterized by a strong backbeat and variations on syncopated instrumental phrases.

Sopra . . . . "Over". Usually used to indicate which hand plays over top of the other in a crossed-hands section.

Subito . . . . Suddenly.

Shuffle . . . . Named after the tap dancing style where the dancer, wearing soft-soled shoes, "shuffles" their feet in a swung 8ths rhythm. Examples include: *KC Shuffle, All Shook Up*

Soul . . . . An African-American style combining elements of gospel music and rhythm and blues. Examples include: *Lapping It Up*

Swing . . . . A fun, dance-like style, usually using swung 8ths. Examples include: *Puffed Up*

Swung 8ths . . . . 8th notes that are written normally, but played in a relaxed triplet rhythm:

Syncopation . . . An emphasis on weak beats and/or rests on strong beats to briefly change the pattern of metrical accents normally found in a time signature. This word is sometimes used to mean "offbeat".

Tango . . . . A rhythmically strict style, with no off-beat and a snare roll on beat 4. Examples include: *Tango of the Desert*

Waltz . . . . A dance in 3/4 time, usually played with a strong accent on the first beat, with weaker beats on counts 2 and 3 in the accompaniment. Examples include: *Sunny Disposition*